MW01240995

Better

MY LIFE. GOD'S DESIGN.

STEPHEN MARTIN

Unless otherwise indicated, all Scripture quotations are taken from the King James Version of the Bible. Public Domain.

Scripture quotations marked AMP are taken from The Amplified Bible. Old Testament copyright © 1987 by Zondervan Corporation. New Testament copyright © 1987 by the Lockman Foundation. Used by permission.

Scripture quotations marked ESV are taken from The Holy Bible, English Standard Version, copyright © 2001 by Crossway Bibles, a publishing ministry of Good News Publishers. Used by permission. All rights reserved.

Scripture quotations marked MSG are taken from The Message, copyright © 2002. Used by permission of NavPress Publishing Group. All rights reserved.

Scripture quotations marked NIV are taken from The Holy Bible: New International Version®, copyright © 1984 and 2011 by International Bible Society, Zondervan Publishing House. Used by permission. All rights reserved.

Scripture quotations marked NKJV are taken from The Holy Bible: New King James Version, copyright © 1982 by Thomas Nelson, Inc. Used by permission. All rights reserved.

Scripture quotations marked NLT are taken from The Holy Bible: New Living Translation, copyright © 2007 by Tyndale House Foundation. Used by permission of Tyndale House Publishers, Inc.

BETTER: MY LIFE. GOD'S DESIGN.

ISBN 978-1-7335699-0-3

Copyright © 2019
One Church Resource
171 FM 3219
Harker Heights, TX 76548
onechurchresource.com

Editor: Linda A. Schantz
Cover & Layout Design: Thomas Ewing, Tim Cross
Illustrations & Study Materials: Rebecca Leach, Kyle Leach, John Morgan

Printed in the United States of America
All rights reserved under International Copyright Law.

Contents and/or cover may not be reproduced in whole or in part in any form without the express written permission of the Publisher. One Church Resource, 171 FM 3219, Harker Heights, TX 76548. *onechurchresource.com*

This book is dedicated to

all those who have helped me become better

over the years, as a Christ-follower,

friend, husband, father, and pastor.

You know who you are, and I am so grateful

for your time and investment in my life.

TABLE OF CONTENTS

HOW TO USE THIS BOOK IN A GROUP SETTING

Take your study to the next level by discussing what you've learned with a group of friends or a small group. You and your friends or group can dig deeper into the better life God has for you and learn how to walk in His design.

To really apply this content to your life you need to bring other people along with you. Discipleship and accountability are the keys to making any spiritual discipline become a living part of your faith walk. As you study the truths contained in **Better: My Life. God's Design.** you'll be able to grow and reach your full potential by surrounding yourself with those whom you can mentor and those who can mentor you.

In the pages that follow each chapter, you'll find devotionals for personal study with Scripture passages, key thoughts, a series of questions for personal reflection, and a journaling section to make this material come alive for you. You may also use these materials to help guide you and your friends in a group discussion about each chapter's topic, using the questions for reflection as a springboard for discussion.

As you study these deeper concepts personally and with trusted friends, you'll be able to take away the principles that will help you grow spiritually and follow God's design for your lives.

Access bonus materials, including small group videos and other resources at *betterplanner.com/book* today!

INTRODUCTION

God's greatest gift to us is the ability to choose. This was the same gift He gave our first parents in the Garden, and the gift of choice was what Jesus bought back for us through His death, burial, and resurrection. God is not a bully, an overlord, or a tyrant. He always gives us a choice.

The journey to *better* always starts with a choice.

As you prepare to embark on this venture to become the person God has designed you to be, it's important for you to make three vital choices.

First is the choice to follow Jesus and live your life His Way. As you prepare to read this book, I want to encourage you. God has a plan for you that is so much bigger and better than you could possibly imagine. He sees you where you are right now, and He says, "I love you, and I want a relationship with you." If you want to be happy, fulfilled, and blessed, I promise you God wants that for you even more than you do. You won't find it your way, but as you follow Jesus and His way, you'll find the better life God has for you.

The second choice you must make is choosing to discover God's vision for your life. My prayer is that you would embrace God's vision fully. He promised if you would seek Him, you would find Him. I pray that as you draw near to Him, He would fill you with purpose and direction, and His vision would compel you forward in ways you've never experienced before. The vision and plan God has for you are so much better than your own dreams and goals. Lean in to Him with your whole heart.

The third choice you must make is the choice to live a disciplined life. The root word for *discipline* is *disciple*. Living God's way and following His vision for your life won't be easy. It will take more grit than talent and more tenacity than luck to achieve it. You'll need discipline to move forward when you don't feel like it, when it would be easier to quit and give up. I pray that you'll persevere in the strength of the Lord.

As I've strived for *better* in my own journey as a Christian, a son, a father, a coach, a friend, and a pastor, I've had to continually come back to these three choices in my life. You will need to do the same. But you can rest assured that as you and I continually make these choices, God is redeeming your past and mine. He's at work in our present here and now, and He's preparing a glorious future where we will be together with Him for eternity.

The goal of this book is that you would become better by embracing God's way. As He gives you vision, purpose, and direction, I pray He will draw you into His perfect plan for your life.

The road to *better* begins and continues with a choice. Choose His better way.

Sincerely,

Stephen Martin

CHAPTER 1

Saved by Grace

Without even talking to you or getting to know you, here's one thing I already know about you: You want to be better. You want to be better today than you were yesterday and better tomorrow than you are today. *(You wouldn't be reading this book if you didn't want that. Would you?)*

You want a better relationship with your family.

You want to be a better friend.

You want a better house.

You want to be a better husband (or wife).

You want to be a better parent.

You want a better paycheck.

You want a better job.

I get it. I want all those things, too. The list of all the better things we want in life goes on and on. Doesn't it?

When we get right down to it, I really believe the core of our desire to advance and move forward comes from a good place. We're not just out to get the best car or the biggest house in the neighborhood or the highest-paying degree. No, for the most part, we want to be better so we can be better for the people in our lives who depend on and love us. When we get better, our families, our children, our friends, our careers, and our churches all get better. As the saying goes, "A rising tide lifts all boats."

It's selfish to want to remain the same. So, what do we do with this burning desire within us?

In our quest for "better" here's what we all do. We start with what we know we need to change. New Year's resolutions? Yes, we've made those. We see that area we need to change. We know it needs some improvement and some focus. We set a goal, and we get to work. We start to hustle. We've all done that. We start changing what we see, what we touch, what we taste, and what we hear. Did you know that's perfectly normal?

"Wow, I need to lose some weight!" If you've thought that before *(and haven't we all thought that at some point or another?!)*, it's pretty predictable what comes next. You're probably going to take a look at changing your diet. You're probably going to try exercising a bit more. You might even get up the courage to go work out at the gym with all the skinny people for a few weeks, or maybe you might even join the Cross Fit or marathoners cults! *(Just joking—well, sort of)* But then what?

Maybe you want that big promotion at work *(more money, more benefits, more chance to make an impact)*. That's a great idea. What are you going to do to get it? You're probably going to head straight to HR or to the Internet to research what you need to get that position. Maybe you're going to take some night classes. Maybe you're going to get your degree or a certificate. Maybe you're going to use your time differently in the office and show your boss you can be counted on to take more responsibility. Good for you! Being a better leader is a worthy goal.

Maybe you want a particular relationship in your life to be better. Maybe it's your spouse or significant other who has grown distant. Maybe there's a friendship you want to restore, or one of your kids is going the wrong direction. What are you going to do? If you're wise *(and I know you are because you're reading this book),* you're going to look at how to make the time to build that relationship back up. I hope you succeed in reaching that loved one or friend before it's too late.

All those things are good, but they don't always work.

Action doesn't always guarantee *better*.

In January, when the holiday pies and cookies are all safely eaten and gone, you've made your resolution to become healthier, eat better, and work out more. You get into the gym, and you're feeling good. But by February or March, you look up one day and realize you haven't been to the gym in a couple weeks. Then weeks become months and months become another year that's passed you by.

THE SECRET

What if I told you I had the secret to getting better in every area of your life, physically, mentally, relationally, and emotionally? What if I told you becoming better wasn't really about you or what you do. You don't have to be the smartest person, the most gifted person, or even a perfect person. Even in times when you didn't know what to do, this secret would guarantee that you'd automatically get better, and you'd finish every New Year's resolution you ever started and achieve every goal you've ever set!

You'd buy my book wouldn't you?

With a secret like this, sales would go through the roof. It wouldn't just be a New York Times' Bestseller. It would be a worldwide, international bestseller!

I have some good news and some bad news. The bad news: I don't have that kind of wisdom. The good news: I know Someone who does, and it isn't even a secret. It's open to all who ask, seek, and knock. The secret to making everything better in life is found in God's Word, the Bible.

Did you know:

In 2017, $9.9 billion dollars was spent by people wanting to get better? This crazy amount of spending has created an entire sector of commerce called the "Self-Help Industry."

With all those billions of dollars being spent, have you looked around at the world lately? Have you turned on your local news station? *Does it seem like we're getting better?*

Every single night on the news, you hear about murder and violent crime. You see sex trafficking out of control. There's poverty, genocide, and hatred all around the world. In the United States alone, nearly forty-five thousand people commit suicide every year. We're shocked regularly as we scroll through our social media feeds only to see another seemingly happy and successful actor, rock star, or high-profile person who has ended his or her life.

Visits to the emergency room for self-inflicted harm are up forty-two percent in just the last ten years. Anxiety disorders affect more than forty million adults in the United States alone. That's eighteen percent of our entire population. And half of that group also suffers from depression. How is that possible?

Look around. We have it all. Don't we? Most of the world lives on two dollars a day. Most of us are not scared of starvation. We're not worried that we're going to be homeless.

Why are we so anxious and depressed? We're worried that we're not good enough and we can't get better. We're worried that no matter how hard we try, we'll never measure up to our expectations and the expectations of others. We're scared of being lonely and insignificant. Some people have completely given up on the idea of *better*.

But even though it may feel like the world around us is getting worse, that's not where we need to stop. We need to set our sights on the truth that we have to believe if we're ever going to get better. It's a truth that can be hard to swallow, especially for the self-reliant, "I'll-make-it-happen," do-it-yourselfer.

Here's the truth: You can't make yourself better.

Even though we may want to get better, and we may even take the steps to make it happen, we just can't do it on our own.

Why is that? Because our concept of *better* isn't good enough. It isn't big enough. It isn't powerful enough to change us. Why do we try so hard and not get better? Because *our better* starts with *US*.

Here's what God's Word says about that:

> **There is a way that appears to be right, but in the end it leads to death.**
>
> **Proverbs 14:12 NIV**

What man thinks is right doesn't lead to *better*.

I grew up in a small town in rural Oklahoma called Mannford. I have a twin sister and an older brother. My dad left us sometime around when I was seven, and, after that, my mom had to raise three kids all alone. I remember the struggle. I saw how hard she tried, how hard she worked, and even as a young boy I remember thinking... *There's got to be something better.* I didn't know Jesus then. I didn't have a relationship with God. But even before I knew God, I knew there was something better. Life wasn't supposed to go that way.

The truth is that God did have something better for me, and He has something so much better for all of us.

> For my thoughts are not your thoughts, neither are your ways my ways... As the heavens are higher than the earth, so are my ways higher than your ways and my thoughts than your thoughts.

> Isaiah 55:8-9 NIV

Did you know you were created for more—for *better*? Better than you're experiencing today, better than you can imagine now and better than the promises of the culture around us. To discover this, we need to go back to the beginning, to the moment when *better* exited our world.

OUR FIRST PARENTS

There's an account in Genesis that tells us when *better* went out the window. It was when our parents (our first ancestors), Adam and Eve traded *better* for *worse*. They walked away from God. They determined in their own hearts that they knew better, and somehow God was holding out on them. They disobeyed God's instruction.

> But you must not eat from the tree of the knowledge of good and evil, for when you eat from it you will certainly die.

> Genesis 2:17 NIV

If you read further you realize that after they ate of the fruit, they realized they were naked, but they didn't just drop dead on the spot right there in the middle of the Garden of Eden. Even though there was a death there that happened, their physical bodies kept going. This used to confuse me as a young man reading the Bible.

It wasn't until I read a story in the book of John about when Jesus encountered a man named Nicodemus that I fully understood what happened in that garden.

Maybe you know the story, Nicodemus was a religious guy, a good guy. He was just trying to be better at following what was right every day. But no matter how good he was or how many rules he followed, he knew there was something more. He knew he was missing something.

He learned about this person named Jesus. Nicodemus heard about the miracles Jesus did and His teaching of a new and better way to live, and Nicodemus was determined to get some answers to the longing in his heart. He went to see Jesus during the night, and this is what happened:

> He [Nicodemus] came to Jesus at night and said, "Rabbi, we know that you are a teacher who has come from God. For no one could perform the signs you are doing if God were not with him."
>
> Jesus replied, "Very truly I tell you, no one can see the kingdom of God unless they are born again."
>
> "How can someone be born when they are old?" Nicodemus asked. "Surely they cannot enter a second time into their mother's womb to be born!"
>
> John 3:2–4 NIV

Did you know that there is something worse than physical death? It wasn't Adam and Eve's physical bodies that died on that day in the Garden. It was their spirits that died right there on the spot. Meaning that they lived with this longing in their hearts for *better*, but they could never reach it because of their separation from God. Their ability to connect to Him, and their ability to get better on their own died in that garden. Their bodies died later. **From that day on, every human born on this planet is born in a state where our bodies are alive, but our spirits are dead.**

Our only chance at *better*, was lost because of sin.

> Therefore, just as sin entered the world through one man [Adam], and death through sin, and in this way death came to all people, because all sinned—
>
> Romans 5:12 NIV [Author's Note]

You and I were created for *better*, but we can't get there by ourselves because of sin.

WHERE ARE WE GOING?

We all want to go somewhere better in life, but if we don't know where we're starting from, it's difficult to get to where we want to go.

I could want to go to Disney World in Orlando, Florida, for a vacation with my family. I could pack everybody up in my car tomorrow and get my wife, Kyla, and the kids all excited about our trip. "We're going to go see Mickey Mouse! Yay!" The girls would have their Mickey ears and princess dresses on. Our baby boy would have his Mickey bib, and we'd all be so happy. My family would cheer as we headed down the road.

But if I drove onto I-35 from our house in Central Texas and headed north, do you know what would happen? It wouldn't be long before Kyla would say something like, "Honey, do you know where you're going?" *(Now, Kyla is really smart because, not only is she a medical doctor, she's also a dedicated follower of directions and reader of maps!)* It wouldn't take long before she'd ask me what I was doing.

I could say all day long, "All roads lead to Disney World," but the fact is, all roads *DON'T* lead to Disney World. Some roads lead to Oklahoma! That's where going north on I-35 from my house leads. If I get in my car without knowing where I'm starting from and using Google Maps, I'm going to end up somewhere I don't want to go.

Many people spend their whole lives like that. They don't know where they're starting from, and they don't understand why the longing in their hearts to be better seems so unattainable. They end up wasting a lot of time and energy starting and stopping, and starting and stopping. And they end up going a little way down the road, but in all different directions.

You can't get to *better* by just wishing to go there or saying you're going to get better with a New Year's resolution. You can't get to *better* on your own.

Why?

Better isn't in you. It's in Jesus.

> **For all have sinned and fall short of the glory of God, and all are justified freely by his grace through the redemption that came by Christ Jesus.**
>
> **Romans 3:23–24 NIV**

This is so important.

The starting place for you, for *better*, is to put your faith in the grace of Jesus. The Bible says that when we put our faith in Jesus, our spirits, which were dead, become alive in Christ. They are born again.

That's what Jesus was telling Nicodemus.

> **Jesus replied, "Very truly I tell you, no one can see the kingdom of God unless they are born again."**
>
> **John 3:3 NIV**

Better begins with our relationship with Jesus—with our being "born again."

The place we all need to start from on the road to *better* is having a life-giving relationship with Jesus—a born again moment where we give Him ownership of our lives.

EASY AS A–B–C

As a young boy, one of the first things I learned when I was learning to read and write was the A-B-C song. It's easy to remember, and it rhymes. I'll have to admit that even sometimes today, on the rare occasion when I have to file something or look something up, that song comes back to me, "Q–R–S–T–U–V–W... *That's right; W comes after V...*" That little song makes it simple.

Some people make things so complicated. But because of Christ's sacrifice, He made getting better easy. We don't have to struggle and work for our own salvation. No, Jesus made becoming a Christ-follower simple. His grace is a free gift to us when we accept Him as our Lord and Savior.

Anytime we want to go from where we are (not so great) to where God wants us to be (better and beyond), we just need to remember A–B–C.

A—Admit

Admit you need God. If you haven't accepted Christ in your heart, your spirit is dead. *(No judgment. That's where we all start from.)*

For *ALL* have sinned and fall short of the glory of God....

Romans 3:23 NIV [Author's Emphasis]

For "all" have sinned, not some. We all made the same decision Adam made in the Garden of Eden. Do you know what the decision was? It was to trade God's best for what we thought was best, which only ends up in us being unfulfilled and striving our entire lives.

We all made that decision to walk away from God at some point. If you haven't already come back, admit that you need Him today. You can't get better apart from Him.

B—Believe

Put your faith in God's plan for better. Better was bought for you and me on the cross when Jesus died for our sins. He came to give us a life that is better— not just here and now, but for all eternity. Better now and better forever.

The thief comes only to steal and kill and destroy; I have come that they may have life, and have it to the full [a life that is better].

John 10:10 NIV [Author's Paraphrase]

We have to admit where we are without Jesus. We have to believe in the power of the cross and the resurrection, but it's not enough to just to think about it. We can't "will" our way into a relationship with Him. We have to do one more thing to get better.

C—Confess

It isn't enough to just believe, the Bible says you have to say what you believe with your mouth. We have to give ownership of our lives to God.

Because if you confess with your mouth that Jesus is Lord and believe in your heart that God raised him from the dead, you will be saved.

Romans 10:9 ESV

God's a perfect gentleman. He's not going to bully His way into your life. He has to be invited to come in. That's what confessing your belief is all about. It's not going through a list of sins you've committed throughout your life. Confession is saying out loud that Jesus is your Lord. He has control of your life. Then you will be born again to live a new life in Him. Then *better* is within your reach.

For you and me to live better, we have to begin with God's way. We must choose a better way—the way that is only made possible through making Jesus your Lord and Savior.

(If you have not accepted Jesus as your Savior, I encourage you to hold your place in this chapter right now, and pray the prayer for salvation found in the back of this book.)

KEY THOUGHT
Better isn't in us.
It's in Jesus.

CHAPTER NOTES

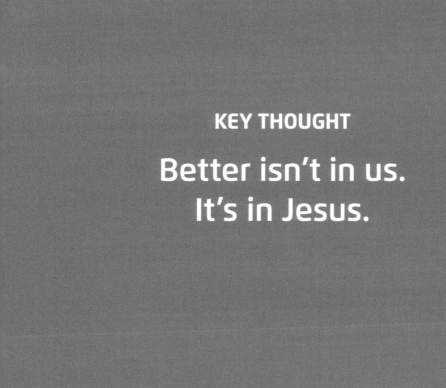

KEY THOUGHT

Better isn't in us.
It's in Jesus.

CHAPTER 1

Saved by Grace

SMALL GROUP AND DEVOTIONAL LESSONS

READ

No matter how hard you try, you can't really make yourself *better*. Your concept of better isn't good enough. It isn't big enough or powerful enough to change you. **As long as you're only looking at what you can do, you can never have the better life God designed for you.**

Adam and Eve thought they could make themselves better, and they listened to a lie from the enemy. This big lie is the same today as it was back then. *"You can do something on your own, apart from God, to get better."*

But that way of thinking only brings sin and destruction.

Thank God there is a better way. God sent His Son, Jesus, to die on a cross to pay the price for the sin and destruction each of us brought upon ourselves. Today, if you will accept Christ and let Him give you His grace, He will give you a new born-again spirit and lead you to the plan He made for you from the beginning of time.

You were created for more—for a better life as God's child.

☐ **DAY 1**   **Genesis 1–3 and John 1**

☐ **DAY 2**   **2 Corinthians 5 and John 2**

☐ **DAY 3**   **Luke 5 and John 3**

☐ **DAY 4**   **Luke 6 and John 4**

☐ **DAY 5**   **Romans 1–2 and John 5**

☐ **DAY 6**   **Romans 3–4 and John 6**

☐ **DAY 7**   **Romans 5 and John 7**

REFLECT

1. What are some areas in your life where you want to be better? Have you had success trying to better yourself on your own?

2. Does God want you to have good behavior or a changed heart? According to the Bible, how can we have lasting change that actually makes us better?

WRITE

Journal your thoughts from the discussion questions here.

CHAPTER 2

Spirit Empowered

Do you remember that day in middle school when the gym teacher picked two team captains for a game, and they lined everybody up to pick teams? Do you remember how you felt standing there waiting for your name to be called?

If I'm being honest, I was never the most athletic kid. That moment terrified me. It was like I was screaming inside, *Pick me! Pick me! PLEASE pick me!*

I stood there hoping to hear my name called before the guy standing next to me.... I had a bad feeling in the pit of my stomach while they picked John, and Eric, and Kyle, and—Heaven forbid—they picked a girl before they picked me! That was embarrassing!

Maybe you weren't like me. Maybe you were always picked first because you're super athletic. Or maybe you were always dead last....

I sure don't miss those days at all! It makes me sweat just thinking about it!

Why? Because nobody wants to go through life as the last person picked. Nobody wants to be a loser!

We all stand around in life wanting to be picked, thinking, *Man, I just want to be better.*

I want to be better than the guy in the next office so that I can get the promotion.

I want my yard to look better than my next-door neighbor's yard.

I want to look younger, be thinner, and be better tomorrow than I am today.

It's too bad that *wanting* to be better and actually *becoming* better are not the same thing.

Remember our key thought from the last chapter: **Better isn't something we can achieve on our own because *better* isn't in us. It's in Jesus.** God's *better* is different than ours.

> **As the heavens are higher than the earth, so are my ways higher than your ways and my thoughts than your thoughts.**
>
> Isaiah 55:9 NIV

CHANGING OUR "WANT TO"

I remember when I first decided to follow Jesus. It was as if my "want to" changed. I wanted to grow and to be better. I wanted to get to know Jesus, and I had a new-found desire to follow God that I didn't have before. I was "born again" (John 3:3). As I started to take steps to grow in my faith, I quickly realized that I had so much to learn. There was so much about this new life I had yet to discover.

One of the things I noticed right away was actually something I didn't expect. Even though my "want to" changed and my desires began to turn toward God, there were some habits, hang ups, and sinful tendencies that still remained even after I was born again. I knew I was saved, yet I still struggled with sin.

In an effort to make things right, I started striving and trying to change myself to get better.

I put all my effort into focusing on my behavior, what I could see, touch, feel, and connect to with my natural senses. It was as if I was focused on curing the symptoms, but I was missing the root cause of my sin.

I mentioned before that my wife, Kyla, is a medical doctor. She sees patients all day who have this same tendency. They come in wanting a quick fix for their symptoms. They want her to make it all go away. They want to get a pill and go home cured. To be honest, many of them couldn't care less about what's really causing their problems. They just want to deal with their immediate physical issues without getting to the root of the problem.

The Bible shows us how different we are from God in our thinking.

> **...For the Lord does not see as man sees; for man looks at the outward appearance, but the Lord looks at the heart.**
>
> 1 Samuel 16:7 NKJV

While we're focused on the outside, God is looking at the inside. He transforms us from the inside out.

As the pastor of a church, one of the greatest privileges I have is to spend time with hurting people. They're so hungry to learn about God, and I get to comfort and encourage them. When they come into my office, it's usually because some kind of crisis or intense situation is going on. *(Hardly anyone comes in just to say "hi.")* As I listen to their stories, inevitably somewhere in the conversation there's a pause when they want me to say something. I love responding with this question: **"Why are you valuable?"**

Nearly every time, that will surprise them. Then I'll wait a couple of seconds for dramatic effect and ask again, **"Why are**

you valuable? Is it because of your job? Your company? Your money? Your looks?"

At that point, almost immediately, I'll get one of two answers.

Some people will puff their chests up and start listing off all of their achievements and accolades. They'll give me all the reasons they shouldn't be going through this problem, or they'll tell me it's someone else's fault that they're in a mess. They'll finish by telling me they are good people, and they're valuable because of what they do.

Other people are more honest. They'll put their heads down in shame and say, "Pastor, I'm not valuable. I'm not valuable because of the things I've done. If you knew what a bad person I was, you wouldn't even want to meet with me."

Fortunately, both of these answers are wrong!

Do you know why you're valuable? It has nothing to do with your job, the car you drive, your bank account balance, or anything you do. It has nothing to do with how good or how bad you've been. In fact, you and I only have value because of one thing. We're created in the image of God.

The best example I can see in the world of this concept is to look at the relationship between a parent and a child.

I love being a father, but, when my children were born, they didn't really add a lot of value to my life. If anything, they actually cost me a lot—a lot of money, time, energy, and sleep!

Kids are really inconvenient and expensive. I love my kids with all my heart, and they're cute, but when they were born, they were completely helpless. My wife and I had to do every single thing for them just for them to survive. And yet we kept having babies. They bring us great joy, and we couldn't imagine life without them. Do you know why my kids have such value to me, even when they mess up or smell bad or break things? It's because when I look into their eyes, I see a reflection of myself.

God is a parent, too. When He looks at you, He doesn't love you any more or less because of what you do. You have value to Him because when He looks at you, He sees Himself reflected back.

Now why does this matter? It matters because when we put value in what we do and how we perform, we miss God's much better path to living up to our full potential. **The secret to our value is found in understanding how God made us.**

GOD'S DESIGN

You can never become better until you follow God's design for your life.

When you look at your son or your daughter, you see little parts of yourself. Your son might have your nose, or your daughter might have your eyes. There are things about us that are also like God.

Did you know God is three parts? He's one God, but He's represented in three unique Persons: God the Father, God the Son, and God the Holy Spirit. And in His image, we're also created in three parts. That's God's design.

> **May God himself, the God of peace, sanctify you through and through. May your whole spirit, soul and body be kept blameless at the coming of our Lord Jesus Christ.**
>
> 1 Thessalonians 5:23 NIV

We are all created in the image of God with three distinct parts:

» **Spirit**—This is the part of us from which we connect with God. When you give your life to Christ, your spirit is born again and made alive.

» **Soul**—This part of you is made up of your mind, your will, and your emotions.

» **Body**—This is how we interact with the world through our five senses.

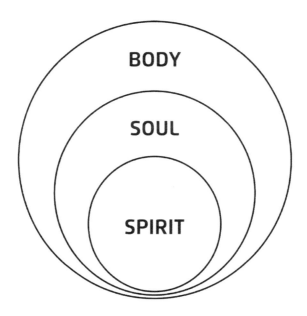

I am a spirit. I have a soul. I live in a body.

To get better, we have to start with our spirits. But because God designed us as three-part beings, we must also deal with our souls and our bodies, too. Once we're born again, it's often our souls that hold us back from lasting success.

Let me illustrate how this works. I mentioned before that my dad left our family when I was only seven years old. His abandoning our family left me with a broken inner image—a broken truth about myself and God as a loving Heavenly Father.

A few years ago, my pastor encouraged me to go to a professional counselor. The counselor helped me to see that the way I related to God and others was pretty much determined by the time I was five to seven years old. I gave my life to Jesus when I was eleven, but long before that, the thinking I had about

God and other people was wrong. Because of those misbeliefs, as a grown man, I was still self-sabotaging areas of my life. These weren't issues with my spirit because my spirit was born again, but my mind, will, and emotions needed some change. At first when I went to see the therapist, I felt a little self-conscious and crazy, but then I realized Paul felt exactly the same way about his own life at times.

The Apostle Paul wrote roughly two-thirds of the New Testament, and here's what he said about his struggle between his spirit and soul.

> **I do not understand what I do. For what I want to do I do not do, but what I hate I do.**
>
> **Romans 7:15 NIV**

LETTING THE SPIRIT LEAD

If even the Apostle Paul struggled with this issue, how can we make lasting changes in our souls so that we can have the better life God designed for us?

Where do we start?

Here's our key thought for lasting life change: Becoming better starts with letting our spirits lead us.

Once we're born again, our spirits can be empowered by God's Holy Spirit inside us, and, instead of letting our emotions and our flesh lead us, we can walk in the fruit of the Spirit.

> **But the fruit of the Spirit is love, joy, peace, patience, kindness, goodness, faithfulness, gentleness, self-control.... If we live in the Spirit, let us also keep in step with the Spirit.**
>
> **Galatians 5:22–23, 25 ESV**

If we want to achieve the better life God has for us, the Bible gives us instruction on three key elements we have to incorporate into our lives to empower God's Spirit to lead our spirits.

1. **God**—You'll never become all that God has called you to be apart from Him. This is the first relationship that leads us to *better*.

    Jesus replied, "Very truly I tell you, no one can see the kingdom of God unless they are born again."

    John 3:3 NIV

2. **God's People**—When you were born again, you were also born into a family. You'll never be all you're called to be apart from the family of God. You need other believers to help you on your journey to becoming better.

    Now you are the body of Christ, and each one of you is a part of it.

    1 Corinthians 12:27 NIV

3. **God's Mission**—We have to be engaged in God's mission. We have to seek and put His kingdom above our own desires and plans. We can't get to *better* if we're on the wrong path. God's mission is the right path to take us to *better*.

    But seek first his kingdom and his righteousness, and all these things will be given to you as well.

    Matthew 6:33 NIV

Our relationship with God, our being connected to His people, and being engaged in His mission are the key factors that will help us to become better.

If we were to illustrate this, it might look something like this:

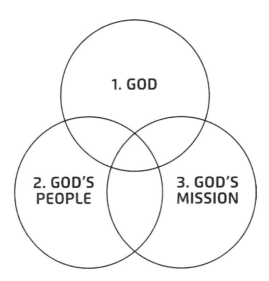

The first circle represents when you say "yes" to God and being born again. The second circle represents your place in God's family. You may not have realized that when you came to Christ a lot of people became your relatives, but no one is born without a family. And the third circle represents your commitment to God's kingdom and expanding His family.

Better exists where these three circles intersect.

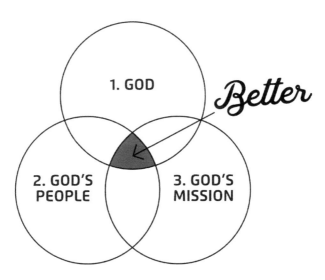

Better is found right in the center of it all.

Better starts from the inside—in your spirit, but it gets worked out through you working with God's people to fulfill His mission. Christianity lived alone is not Christianity at all. Your Christianity is personal, but it's not private. I am so grateful that Jesus Christ saved me, but it was His power working in other believers that redeemed my life.

God wants to do incredible things in and through you, and that starts by letting His Spirit empower your spirit, which will lead you right into the center of His will. You can't get to *better* if you're trying to resist your flesh (your soul and body) in your own power. That's why Jesus sent the Holy Spirit as our Helper. We must choose to follow the Holy Spirit, and let Him empower our lives.

Do you remember the "WWJD" bracelets people used to wear? (*WWJD* stood for *What Would Jesus Do?*.) They were effective because they caused people to stop and consider Jesus' way before doing things. We need a bracelet that reminds us that being led by our spirits is the better way! We only have one real choice when it comes to defeating the power of sin and temptation. We must choose the spirit over the flesh. When we're led by the spirit, the resulting fruit is freedom (not death)!

The flesh *feels* better, but being led by your spirit *IS* better! Jesus invites us to appeal to a better nature and to let our spirits be empowered by the Spirit of God. The Holy Spirit lives in us to show us a better way!

KEY THOUGHT
Becoming better starts with letting your spirit lead.

CHAPTER NOTES

Becoming better
starts with letting your
spirit lead.

CHAPTER 2

Spirit Empowered

SMALL GROUP AND
DEVOTIONAL LESSONS

READ

Wanting to be better and actually *becoming* better are not the same thing. Better isn't something we can achieve on our own. The better life you seek only comes God's way. His ways are so much higher than our ways. Even when we become born again, we still struggle with the effects of sin in our flesh. Old habits die hard.

The key to learning how to shake off these old patterns and sinful desires is to realize that you can never become better until you understand God's original design for your life. You were created in three parts: spirit, soul, and body. **Even though your spirit is recreated in the righteousness of Christ and the image of God, your soul (your mind, will, and emotions) and your body (your senses) can hold you back from lasting success.**

God doesn't change you from the outside in—by you doing good things or looking good on the outside. You can only be changed from the inside out. **When you let the Holy Spirit empower your born-again spirit, He will lead you right into the center of His will.** Being led by your spirit is the only way to take control of those old patterns of your flesh and get to the better life God designed for you.

☐ **DAY 1**   **Romans 6 and John 8**

☐ **DAY 2**   **Romans 7 and John 9**

☐ **DAY 3**   **Romans 8 and John 10**

☐ **DAY 4**   **Galatians 5:1–12 and John 11**

☐ **DAY 5**   **Galatians 5:13–26 and John 12**

☐ **DAY 6**   **Ephesians 6:10–20 and John 13**

☐ **DAY 7**   **1 Corinthians 10:11–13 and John 14**

REFLECT

1. What part of you (spirit, soul, or body) needs to change first in order to have the better life God has planned for you? Why does *inside-out* change work but *outside-in* doesn't?

2. Who helps us take control of the negative patterns we have been living in? What does it mean to be led by the Holy Spirit?

WRITE

Journal your thoughts from the discussion questions here.

_____

_____

_____

_____

_____

_____

_____

_____

_____

_____

_____

_____

_____

_____

CHAPTER 3

Driven by Faith

I would guess since you're reading a Christian book, you'd consider yourself to be a person of faith. But let's not assume anything—maybe you aren't so sure. You don't know if you really believe in all this God stuff, but someone gave you this book, and you wanted to check it out. Or maybe you are a person of faith, but you know somebody you've tried to talk to about God, and they've said, "Thanks, but I'm not really a person of faith."

Here's a little truth you should know: Everyone is a person of faith. Everybody is a true believer.

The question is: Faith in what? and a believer in whom?

What you have faith in determines your future.

God has designed us as human beings to be driven by faith.

So, what is faith? The dictionary defines *faith* as *trust or confidence in someone or something.*

What or whom do you trust and have confidence in?

Much of what you believe about God, yourself, and others is a product of your experience. Maybe because of things that happened with your family, or because of a difficult season, you learned to believe things that helped you make it through hard times, but today those beliefs are ultimately holding you back from God's best.

It's possible to be saved and to be going to Heaven, but to have a life of Hell on Earth. We might believe that God wants it to be that way because it helps us explain our troubles away, but that's wrong. That's not God's plan. Absolutely, He wants to give us lives that are better in Heaven, but He also wants us to have the best lives now.

> **The thief comes only to steal and kill and destroy; I have come that they may have life, and have it to the full.**
>
> **John 10:10 NIV**

THE VOICES IN YOUR HEAD

Our minds are constantly fighting suspicions, doubts, insecurities, and fears that somehow God doesn't want us to have a good life now. All kinds of crazy thoughts can and will swirl through our minds on any given day. Thoughts such as:

Is my marriage going to make it?

Am I going to get fired?

Are my kids going to turn out OK?

How am I going to pay these bills?

Am I going to fail just like my mom and dad always said I would?

Do I really have what it takes?

These thoughts don't come from your born-again spirit. They come from your enemy—the devil.

This may sound crazy, but there *literally* are voices inside your head. You can choose to lean in to the voice of God, or you can believe the lies of the enemy.

Every day there is a very real fight happening. If we act on those lies, we aren't being empowered by our spirits. We're living out of what the Bible calls, "the flesh." You and I only have two choices when it comes to what we're going to believe. We can believe the Spirit, which gives life, or we can believe the flesh which produces death and decay.

According to the Apostle Paul, we have a choice. We can either take those thoughts from the enemy captive, or they will take us captive.

> **The mind governed by the flesh is death, but the mind governed by the Spirit is life and peace.**
>
> **Romans 8:6 NIV**

We have to lock those voices inside our heads up and replace the lies with truths about God from His Word. If you let your mind be governed by false beliefs planted by the enemy, you'll never have peace and the better life God wants for you. The devil is trying to rob you of the joy of living in God's truth, and he uses lies to convince you that you can't walk in everything the Word of God promises.

Basically, our thoughts are either rooted in the flesh or in the Spirit.

Again, what you believe about God and yourself determines your future.

> **...He was a murderer from the beginning, not holding to the truth, for there is no truth in him. When he lies, he speaks his native language, for he is a liar and the father of lies.**
>
> **John 8:44 NIV**

The enemy's only weapon against us is a lie! He tells us lies about God, lies about ourselves, lies about the future, and lies about other people.

To defeat Satan's lies and walk in God's best for your life, you have to change the way you think and align your beliefs with the Bible. You can't just start by changing your behavior. You have to replace the lies with the truths found in Scripture.

I love what the Bible says about itself. It says that it's sharper than any double-edged sword (Hebrews 4:12). It cuts right between the things of the soul and the things of the spirit. It helps us to tell the difference between fact and fiction, between lies and the truth. God's Word gives us faith (Romans 10:17). The Bible is your filter. It's going to show you what to believe, what to trust in, and what to walk away from. It's going to give you the core principles you need to know and believe about God so that you can have a firm foundation for the better life He's designed for you.

7 TRUTHS WE SHOULD BELIEVE ABOUT GOD

Because much of what we believe comes from our personal experiences, many of which happened before we were born again, it's important to correct these lies and false beliefs and not allow them to continue to wreak havoc in our lives. **It isn't enough to just resist or ignore a lie, you have to replace the lie with a truth,** a truth about God and His plan for you.

Here are seven biblical truths to replace the most common lies we believe about God and ourselves.

1. **God's plan for me is better than my plan for me.**

   "For I know the plans I have for you," declares the Lord, "plans to prosper you and not to harm you, plans to give you hope and a future."

   Jeremiah 29:11 NIV

Many people really struggle with this question: *Does God want me to be happy?* The answer is "yes." He wants you to be happy. I grew up around church, and oftentimes I heard really religious people say something like, "God doesn't want you to be happy. He wants you to be holy." The last part is true, but the first part is nonsense! I've never been happier in my life than when I'm following Jesus. It's Jesus who makes you holy, and Jesus also wants you to be happy. We are most happy when we are following His plan for our lives, not when we're chasing feelings and emotions, which change like the shifting seas.

2. God's plan is higher and bigger than me.

As the heavens are higher than the earth, so are my ways higher than your ways and my thoughts than your thoughts.

Isaiah 55:9 NIV

I can't tell you how many times I've walked through a difficult situation thinking I had all the facts and I understood exactly what was going on, only to realize God had a different perspective. While I was going through a trial, I thought one thing, but as I got away from it a little bit, I saw how God protected me or used the situation to have a great impact on someone else. We have to believe God's plan is bigger than us. We need to trust that His perspective is so much higher than ours, and He wastes nothing in developing us.

3. God's plan for me starts with me.

...I have set before you life and death, blessings and curses. Now choose life, so that you and your children may live.

Deuteronomy 30:19 NIV

God gave you the right to choose His plan. No one controls your future. Every day you have a choice of whom you're going to serve. No one holds your destiny in their hands except God, but God puts the decision to walk in it into your hands.

4. God has me right where He wants me.

The Lord is my Shepherd, I lack nothing. He makes me lie down in green pastures, he leads me beside quiet waters, he refreshes my soul. He guides me along the right paths for his name's sake.

Psalm 23:1-3 NIV

I remember early on in my faith, thinking: *Does God even know where I am?* I've walked many people through this struggle—the fear that they're not in the right place. Some people move from church to church, job to job, or even from city to city out of fear. But sometimes the best thing you can do when you don't know what to do is stay put and believe God knows where you are. Plant your feet and be faithful with what He's put into your hands. God has you right where He wants you, and you're positioned to be blessed.

5. God is always on time.

There is a time for everything, and a season for every activity under the heavens.

Ecclesiastes 3:1 NIV

You've heard the saying, "God is never late, but He's seldom ever early." In the gap between our problem and the answer, when we're waiting on God, He's building our faith. We may be thinking, "Help, Lord! Move this mountain now," but what He wants you to do is to build up your strength to climb it. God's timing is perfect. We have to exercise patience and trust that He's always right on time.

6. **God has given me everything I need right now.**

> And my God will meet all your needs according to the riches of his glory in Christ Jesus.
>
> **Philippians 4:19 NIV**

When God calls you to move in a certain direction, He always provides provision. God resources His vision with His provision to meet your needs. (By the way *want* is not the same as *need*.) We have to trust that God has given us everything we need to meet our needs for today so that we'll keep our eyes on Him.

7. **God will finish His work in me if I don't give up.**

> Let us not become weary in doing good, for at the proper time we will reap a harvest if we do not give up.
>
> **Galatians 6:9 NIV**

Many people give up right before their breakthrough. Just before they get to *better*, they quit. They stop trusting God. But the Bible says we'll reap a harvest if we don't quit. Harvests aren't fast. If we will just stay in the game, it won't happen overnight, but it's guaranteed that God will finish His work in us.

If we want to make our lives better, we have to be driven by faith—the complete trust and confidence that what God says about Himself and us is true.

We'll never outgrow this need to reject the enemy's lies and replace them with God's Word. The process of renewing our minds with God's truth is a life-long process. We don't just wake up one day with our souls renewed. That's why it's vital for us to be students of God's Word. The Scriptures have the power to change our lives, if we'll let them.

Better comes from the inside and works its way out of us through right believing and faith in God's goodness.

KEY THOUGHT

What you believe about God and yourself changes everything.

CHAPTER NOTES

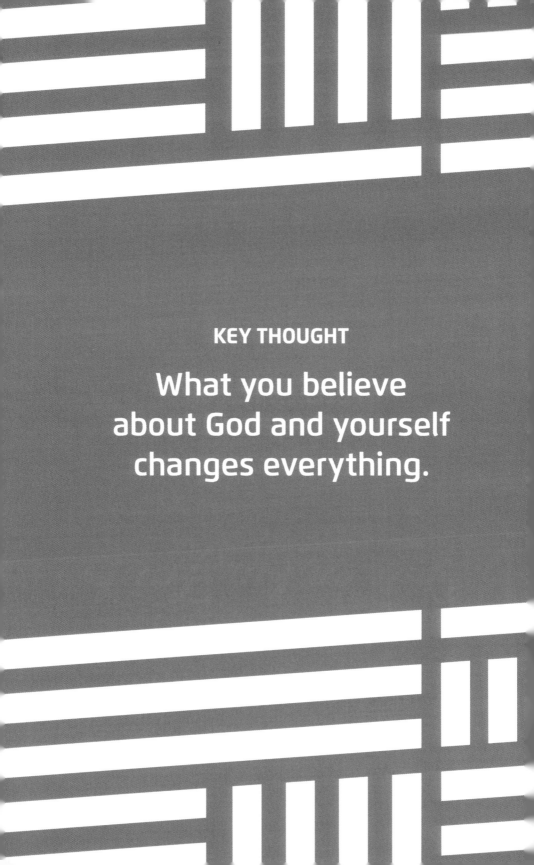

KEY THOUGHT

What you believe
about God and yourself
changes everything.

CHAPTER 3

Driven by Faith

SMALL GROUP AND
DEVOTIONAL LESSONS

READ

What you believe about God, yourself, and others is mostly a product of your experience. Every person fights thoughts of doubt, insecurity, and fear, but those thoughts don't come from God or your born-again spirit. They come from the devil. His only weapon against you is a lie. You don't have to believe him. You have a choice. You can take those thoughts captive with the truth of God's Word and refuse to let doubt overcome you.

Faith in God and His Word overcomes all doubt and fear. **What you believe about God and yourself changes everything.** You must chose to believe that God has a great plan for your life before you can walk in it. God's plan for you is better, higher, and bigger than your own plan. God has you right where He wants you, and He will provide what you need when you need it. You will see God's plan for you come to pass if you don't give up.

God wants to bless you and make you better. He wants to give you His abundant life through Jesus. He has positioned you at the right place at the right time with all the provision you need. Don't fall for the lies of the enemy. Trust God to see you through. Stand firm in faith, and receive the better life God designed for you today.

☐ **DAY 1**   **Romans 12 and John 15**

☐ **DAY 2**   **Philippians 4:4–8 and John 16**

☐ **DAY 3**   **2 Timothy 1:1–7 and John 17**

☐ **DAY 4**   **Proverbs 4:20–23 and John 18**

☐ **DAY 5**   **Ephesians 4:22–32 and John 19**

☐ **DAY 6**   **1 John 1:1–10 and John 20**

☐ **DAY 7**   **Matthew 21:18–22 and John 21**

REFLECT

1. How have your life experiences shaped what you believe about God? How have they shaped what you believe about yourself? Are those negative or positive beliefs?

2. What are some negative thoughts you may have had that you know are not from God? What is the best defense against the lies the devil tells you about God, yourself, and others?

WRITE

Journal your thoughts from the discussion questions here.

CHAPTER 4

Better Together

Do you know what one big difference is between us and God? Of course, there are a lot of differences, but here's a big one:

God sees the big picture in everything. He always plays the long game.

Our tendency is to look at ourselves—what we offer, how we fit, what we have now—but by doing that, we often miss the heart of God, not just for us, but for the entire world—for all people. In fact, the Bible tells us why Jesus is waiting to return to the Earth and make everything on this planet the way it was supposed to be.

> **The Lord is not slow in keeping his promise [to return], as some understand slowness. Instead he is patient with you, not wanting anyone to perish, but everyone to come to repentance.**
>
> **2 Peter 3:9 NIV [Author's Note]**

The reason Jesus doesn't come back riding on a white horse with an army of saints and angels right now is because He's still building something really important and amazing. Do you know what that is?

> Jesus answered... "Upon this rock I will build my church; and the gates of hell shall not prevail against it."
>
> Matthew 16:17–18 KJV

Jesus is building His Church! It may seem like He's taking too long to return, but God's playing the long game. He's waiting for one more person to be born again, one more soul to say "yes" to the Gospel.

The Church is central to us walking in the better life God has planned for us. Jesus builds us through spiritual family—through the local church.

> Consequently, you are no longer foreigners and strangers, but fellow citizens with God's people and also members of his household.
>
> Ephesians 2:19 NIV

Here's a key point: To make us better, God brings us together.

Have you ever heard someone say, "I love God, but I don't like the people in the church."? Or how about, "I love Jesus. I just don't like Christians."? Or, "I'd go to church, if it wasn't full of hypocrites!"?

It's too bad some people feel that way about the Church. That isn't the way God designed it. Maybe you feel that way because of an experience you had at one point in your life that marked you. As we saw in the last chapter, one bad experience can sidetrack your perception of something, and that can affect your entire destiny.

Some people think they can achieve *better* in their lives on their own, apart from the local church, but that's not true. No one can get to *better* on their own. They have to be connected to God. And connecting to God means connecting to His people.

God uses relationships in the local church to redeem the broken parts of our lives.

The Bible describes the Church (both the big "C" universal Church, and the little "c" local church) in two ways. The Bible uses these metaphors to help us understand this concept of what He wants to do in and through us, not just individually, but when He brings us together.

THE CHURCH IS A FAMILY

> Do not rebuke an older man harshly, but exhort him as if he were your father. Treat younger men as brothers, older women as mothers, and younger women as sisters, with absolute purity.
>
> 1 Timothy 5:1–2 NIV

A family is a group of people who operate primarily on the basis of relationships, not rules. Sure, early in childhood the rules of the house are all about learning to obey and telling your kids what to do. You want what's best for them. But eventually those kids will grow up, and they're going to have to know how to make good decisions. If we build our families on rules, things won't work out well in the end. We can't just send a group email to our adult children, saying "Compliance is not optional." They're not our employees! Families are relational.

The great thing about family is that everything and everyone you need is around the table. If you want a better life, you need to realize it's connected to your relationships.

Your destiny is tied to your relationships. Relationships determine your future! God designed the church relationally to give us a great advantage and to make us all better!

The church is a spiritual family, and just like any natural family, a healthy family is made up of at least three generations.

Maybe you're older. You may think that people have forgotten you, that the younger generation has left you behind, but that's not true. We need you as spiritual coaches and mentors, our spiritual moms, dads, aunts, and uncles. We need your wisdom.

Maybe you're at the opposite end of the age spectrum. You're younger, and maybe you feel as if nobody wants to hear your opinion or what you have to say. But that's not true, either. We need you, too. A healthy family needs brothers, sisters, sons, and daughters. You're the life and energy behind God's design for His family, the local church.

No matter what your age or background, we all need deep spiritual friendships, the people who come alongside us and encourage us to become better. We all need godly friends to help keep us accountable.

> **Long, long ago he decided to adopt us into his family through Jesus Christ. (What pleasure he took in planning this!)**
>
> **Ephesians 1:5 MSG**

Did you catch that? God took great pleasure in putting you into His family. He didn't make a mistake. We make mistakes, but God doesn't. He places you in a local church for a reason.

THE CHURCH IS A BODY

The Church functions as **one body** on the basis of our individual spiritual gifts and character.

> **Just as our bodies have many parts and each part has a special function, so it is with Christ's body. We are many parts of one body, and we all belong to each other.**
>
> **Romans 12:4-5 NLT**

Every family and every physical body has a structure. The structure of the family provides security and protection. The structure of the body (the bones, muscles, tissues, and organs) does the same.

Not too long ago I was taking my daughter to school, and it was pouring rain. I pulled out an umbrella to keep her covered, and I thought to myself, *Wow! An umbrella is a great picture of how the structure of the local church functions.* When you pop open an umbrella in a storm, all of a sudden, you're shielded. Similarly, there's a spiritual covering for you in the local church so that God's design for your life can be reinforced, and you'll be secure in your faith.

Jesus gave special ministry gifts in the Church to some people. They're similar to a spiritual umbrella. Not everyone has these gifts, but the leadership of the local church does. They are part of the structure of the Body of Christ to provide its members with more strength and protection. Putting yourself under a covering of spiritual authority will bring blessing and accountability to your life.

The Apostle Paul wrote about these special leadership gifts.

> **Now these are the gifts Christ gave to the church: the apostles, the prophets, the evangelists, and the pastors and teachers. Their responsibility is to equip God's people to do his work and build up the church, the body of Christ.**
>
> **Ephesians 4:11-12 NLT**

It's the responsibility of the people with these leadership gifts to equip God's people to use their spiritual giftings to build up the Church.

If you want to get to God's plan for *better* in your life, **you have to be connected to God's family, using your spiritual gifts, doing His work as a member of His body.**

Do you remember in the last chapter we were studying about not believing the devil's lies about God and ourselves?

Here's a big lie: You can be all that God wants you to be apart from the Church.

It simply isn't true. Why? Because Christ loves His Church, and He gave up His life to build it. **The Church is a really big deal.**

You'll only fail alone.

To make us better, God brings us together.

It's in relationships—in His family, as a part of His Body—that we're made into the image of Jesus. **You and I... we're better together.**

KEY THOUGHT
To make us better, God brings us together.

CHAPTER NOTES

KEY THOUGHT

To make us better, God brings us together.

CHAPTER 4

Better Together

SMALL GROUP AND DEVOTIONAL LESSONS

READ

No one can become better on their own. You have to be connected to God, and being connected to God means connecting to His people. **Jesus only promised to build one thing on the Earth, and that's His Church.** Every believer must be a part of a local church in order to thrive and live in the better life God designed for them.

The Church is a family that operates on the basis of relationships, not rules. Your destiny is tied to your relationships. If you want a better life, it's connected to your relationships with a spiritual family. God took great pleasure in placing you into His family. He wants you to take your place as an active member of a local church.

The Church is also a body. It functions on the basis of spiritual gifts and character with each member doing his or her part. The structure in a local church provides you with security and protection. **You can never become all that God wants you to be apart from His Church.** It's only when you are connected to His family in a local body of believers that you can be made into the image of Jesus.

- ☐ **DAY 1**   **1 Corinthians 12:12–31 and Acts 1**

- ☐ **DAY 2**   **Romans 12:4–5 and Acts 2**

- ☐ **DAY 3**   **Ephesians 4:1–4 and Acts 3**

- ☐ **DAY 4**   **Ephesians 2:19–22 and Acts 4**

- ☐ **DAY 5**   **Romans 12:6–8 and Acts 5**

- ☐ **DAY 6**   **Ephesians 4:11–13 and Acts 6**

- ☐ **DAY 7**   **Colossians 1:1–18 and Acts 7**

REFLECT

1. What has your experience been when it comes to connections with others in the church? Would you describe those connections as "family"? How would you describe them?

2. Are you connected to others in the church who help you grow and get better? If not, why do you think that is? How have the people you are connected to helped you grow and find where you belong?

WRITE

Journal your thoughts from the discussion questions here.

_____

_____

_____

_____

_____

_____

_____

_____

_____

_____

_____

_____

_____

_____

CHAPTER 5

Moved by Vision

Did you know you have a super power? You have supernatural eyes. No, not like Superman. Although sometimes it would be nice to have X-ray vision. *(Like when your kids are really quiet. Wouldn't it be nice to be able to see through walls and know what they were up to?)* Or how about having laser vision? There are a few times when the ability to shoot lasers out of your eyes might come in handy! Like when the service tech comes to your house, "What do you mean my Internet is going to be down for three more days?!" *(Laser eyes)* —Zap! He's toast!

Too bad you can't really have X-ray or laser vision, but you can have the supernatural power of God's vision (His design) for your life so that you can become better.

How do you find and follow God's vision for your life? Let's break this down into simple, practical steps and revisit what God said in Isaiah 55:9.

> **As the heavens are higher than the earth, so are my ways higher than your ways and my thoughts than your thoughts.**
>
> **Isaiah 55:9 NIV**

God's design is higher—and better—than what we could plan for ourselves, and He's given us His power—the supernatural power of vision—to walk in it.

Whatever you focus on, you get full of. A vision has the power to compel you to move toward it.

Did you know that vision has done some good, great—and, unfortunately, some horrible things in the world?

» **A Vision for Evil**—It was an evil vision that led Hitler toward his picture of an Aryan Germany and ultimately to the murder of millions of innocent people, mostly Jews, during World War II.

» **A Vision for Good**—It was vision that led Thomas Edison to invent the light bulb, after trying and failing hundreds of times. And the power of vision led Alexander Graham Bell to invent the telephone that others improved upon and turned into "smartphones." *(And now we're all addicted to them night and day!)*

» **A Vision for *Better***—It was vision—seeing and walking in God's design—that led Jesus to the cross and, ultimately, to the resurrection.

> **Fixing our eyes on Jesus, the pioneer and perfecter of faith. *For the joy set before him* he endured the cross, scorning its shame, and sat down at the right hand of the throne of God.**
>
> **Hebrews 12:2 NIV [Author's Emphasis]**

And in following after Jesus, God uses a vision of what life could be to make us better. God has a plan, a personal and individual vision, for every single one of His children to follow.

> **Where there is no vision, the people perish....**
>
> **Proverbs 29:18 KJV**

The *English Standard Version* translation of this verse in the Bible says, without vision, people "cast off restraint." They have no discipline because, without vision, people don't have any purpose.

Vision connects our lives to significance and meaning for the future. Without knowing and following God's design, we can't connect the dots. We can't see how what we're doing now has any importance or bearing on the future.

IF IT FEELS GOOD...

You know, I love donuts. I love cake donuts. I love glazed donuts. I love the big, filled long Johns. I love the ones with sprinkles. I love donuts. But I have a vision for my body that it will be healthy. If I go into the donut shop and stare at the rows and rows of donuts, my vision to stay healthy gets a bit cloudy. But if I resist the urge and look the other way when I'm driving by the donut store, it gets easier to focus on what I really want for my future.

Because of a lack of vision, people spend their whole lives doing what feels good in the moment while missing their deeper, more fulfilling life's purpose. God didn't just design us to resist what's bad. He designed us to walk toward what's better.

With a clear personal vision, you can live with purpose and direction knowing that what you're doing today will make a difference, not just in your life, but in the people's lives all around you. Vision is compelling. It pulls you toward the future.

Do you want to have a better life? Let's look at Proverbs 29:18 in *The Message*.

> If people can't see what God is doing [they
> can't see His vision for their lives], they stumble

> all over themselves; But when they attend to
> what he reveals, they are most blessed.
>
> ### Proverbs 29:18 MSG [Author's Note]

Did you catch that? When you see what God reveals, you are **most blessed** (*better*)!

Here's a truth you need to take to heart: **What you *see* makes you better!**

ASK HIM FOR HIS VISION

When was the last time you stopped and asked God to share His vision for your life?

Having a personal vision based on God's design for your life is essential to personal growth. Without it we miss the things God wants to do in and through us. A vision gives us clarity and keeps us moving forward.

> **...Write the vision and make it plain on tablets,
> That he may run who reads it. For the vision is yet
> for an appointed time....**
>
> ### Habakkuk 2:2 NKJV

> **...Write what you see. Write it out in big block
> letters so that it can be read on the run.**
>
> ### Habakkuk 2:2 MSG

Why big block letters? Because we get distracted. Sometimes as we're walking toward our preferred future, the cares and circumstances of life knock us off course. We need to have a personal vision from God printed in big block letters right in front of us.

God has a unique vision for every one of His kids, and we need to **see it, write it, and run with it!**

What you see makes you better, and it also determines your future. The vision keeps you moving forward.

Probably one of the best examples of this that I've seen is the way things work in the military when a family gets new orders. As I've pastored a church near the army base of Fort Hood, I've watched this happen time and time again. When a person in a military home gets a new assignment, those orders tell them where they're going and what their duties will be when they get there. When those new orders come, the family begins to organize around this new vision for their future. They start to make plans. They strategize how they're going to pack up and move. They begin to research where their kids are going to go to school. The vision keeps the family moving forward and building the details of their new assignment.

As we're building and moving toward the future, it's critical that our vision is built upon God's design for our lives. But sometimes those assignments don't seem as clear as military orders.

How can we be sure that we're following God's vision for our lives? Let's look at some practical steps we can take to find and follow God's vision.

HOW TO FIND GOD'S VISION

Here are some practical steps you can take to find God's vision for your life.

» **Ask God.** To truly know yourself is to know the One who created you. Consult God. Invite Him into the process. He knows you better than you know you.

» **Ask God's people.** Invite others who love God and love you into the process. We talked about this in the last chapter. We can't do this alone. Does your vision have input from the spiritual family God has called you to walk with?

» **Consider God's mission.** Does your vision fit within God's vision? Remember Jesus only promised to build one thing, and it wasn't your personal vision. It was His Church. Does your vision prioritize God's mission on Earth, reaching His lost sons and daughters? Or is it just about you? Does your vision include reaching someone far from God?

> ...Go and make disciples of all nations... teaching them to obey everything I have commanded you....
>
> Matthew 28:19-20 NIV

Remember: God's plan is to do something *in you* so that He can do something *through you.*

HOW TO FOLLOW GOD'S VISION

» **Write it down!** (Habakkuk 2:2) Don't just think about it. *Actually* write it down.

» **Start with the end in mind.** We only have a limited amount of time on this planet to do what God has called us to do. Think about your funeral and consider what your life will have meant to the people closest to you. What do you want them to say about you? What do you want God to say to you when you meet Him? Think about your legacy, and don't get distracted by things that have no eternal impact.

» **Set your top five to seven priorities.** Determine what's most important. God should be at the top of your list, then your spouse, your church, your career, etc. It's not enough to see a picture of what you want your life to be. You have to ask yourself the question: *What are the things that I have to do before I die?* Within your priorities, here are some key principles.

> › **Write down your current reality.** Be brutally honest. Remember, we said in the first chapter that you can't see how to get where you want to go until you know where you're starting from.

> › **Write about the future you see.** Write down a Bible verse to believe and speak over each area of your life: your relationship with God, your family, your spiritual family and friends, your career, your health, your finances, etc. Then speak those scriptures over your circumstances daily. The Word of God becomes alive and active in our lives when it comes out of our mouths. It can keep us on track.

» **Set some goals you can actually accomplish.** I love the acrostic for setting goals that's popular in the business world. Make your goals S–M–A–R–T goals. Your goals should be *Specific, Measurable, Attainable, Realistic, and Time Bound.* Start with something you can reach. Set quarterly goals (something you can do in thirteen weeks), and write them down.

» **Map out your relationships.** If you're going to get to *better* in your life, you need other people to help you achieve your personal vision. Write down every relationship you have. Categorize them, and be intentional about pouring into those relationships. Make a note of areas where you don't have the relationships you need to grow. God wants to fill those gaps.

» **Learn about your unique personality and spiritual gifts.** Knowing how God designed you will help you move toward your vision in a powerful way. It will help you relate to, love, and lead others better.

Don't just move through time from day to day without any direction. If you do, you won't end up where you want to be.

If you want your life to be **better, significant, and important,** fulfill God's design for you, and **harness the supernatural power of vision!**

KEY THOUGHT

What you see makes you better.

CHAPTER NOTES

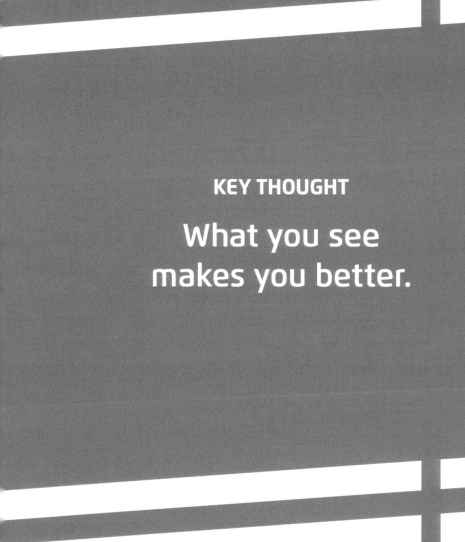

KEY THOUGHT

What you see
makes you better.

CHAPTER 5

Moved by Vision

SMALL GROUP AND DEVOTIONAL LESSONS

READ

God's design for you is better than what you could ever plan for yourself, and He's given you the supernatural power of vision to walk in it. It was vision—the power of walking in God's plan—that led Jesus to the cross and to the resurrection. Jesus stayed focused on the vision and followed it to bring salvation to us.

God has a personal vision for you to follow that connects your life to significance and meaning for the future. Because of a lack of vision, many people spend their whole lives doing what feels good in the moment, and they miss the better life full of purpose that God has for them. But when you see what God reveals and walk in it, you are blessed! What you see makes you better. A vision gives you clarity and keeps you moving forward. It will determine your future. And when you see it, write it, and run with it!

If you haven't seen the vision God has for your life yet, ask Him to show it to you. Test what you see by submitting it to godly people you trust and to the ultimate vision of building God's Church. **His plan is to do something *in you* so He can do something *through you*.** Prioritize what He reveals to you, and you'll walk in the better life God has designed for you.

☐ **DAY 1**   **Proverbs 29:18 and Acts 8**

☐ **DAY 2**   **Psalm 23 and Acts 9**

☐ **DAY 3**   **Habakkuk 2:2–3 and Acts 10**

☐ **DAY 4**   **Psalm 96:9–12 and Acts 11**

☐ **DAY 5**   **Joel 2:28–32 and Acts 12**

☐ **DAY 6**   **Revelation 21:1–5 and Acts 13**

☐ **DAY 7**   **Matthew 6:24–34 and Acts 14**

REFLECT

1. Would you say that you're living your life with vision? If so, what is that vision? If not, what do you think is holding you back?

2. God has a vision for each of our lives. Do you believe your vision lines up with His? What are some things you may need to adjust in order to align yourself with God's vision for your life?

WRITE

Journal your thoughts from the discussion questions here.

CHAPTER 6

A Better Steward

Did you ever notice how, at first glance, some of the things Jesus said don't seem to make much sense?

I know you're probably thinking, *What?! That seems like blasphemy!*

Hold on now! Don't get out your rocks and start throwing them at me! I fully believe everything Jesus said.

All I'm saying is that maybe, at the first impression, some things God said may *seem to be contradictory* to what we think is right.

Think about some of the things Jesus said:

"The first will be last."

"If someone makes you carry their stuff a mile, carry it two."

"If someone slaps you in the face, turn the other cheek, and let him slap you again."

The world would tell you that every single one of those things is wrong. But we need to go back to the Bible, and to our keynote scripture for this book, to see God's explanation.

Let's look at it in *The Message* version of the Bible this time.

> **"I don't think the way you think. The way you work isn't the way I work.... For as the sky soars high above the earth, so the way I work surpasses the way you work, and the way I think is beyond the way you think."**
>
> **Isaiah 55:8–9 MSG**

God's design is so much higher and better than what we could ever have in mind for ourselves, that sometimes we may have trouble understanding His ways. If God's ways are higher, obviously, that means our ways are *lower*.

Our ways might bring us momentary pleasures, but they never fully satisfy us, make us better, or lead us to lives of significance.

Here's another thing Jesus said, and it's the topic we're going to be focusing on in this chapter:

> **Whoever finds their life will lose it, and whoever loses their life for my sake will find it.**
>
> **Matthew 10:39 NIV**

That's an interesting statement. Isn't it?

Jesus may call some of us to give up our lives and go serve in some orphanage in some hidden place in a Third World country or to preach the Gospel as missionaries around the globe. He has called a lot of men and women in the church I pastor to give up their time with their loved ones, and even sometimes their physical lives, to serve in the military so that others in our world can be free. But I believe there's even more to what Jesus said than that.

His ways are better—bigger—higher.

I know what you're thinking: *Pastor, how could Jesus ask me to give more than dying for Him? What more could I possibly give?*

I believe that the "more" and the "better" Jesus is asking us for is not just to die for Him, **but to live for Him.**

If you won't live for Jesus, you will never die for Him.

Jesus wants us to give Him everything. **He's asking us to put all the resources we have—our lives, our time, our abilities, and our finances—on the line for Him and to steward them wisely.**

GOD IS THE OWNER. WE ARE THE MANAGERS.

The words *stewardship* and *steward* aren't something we hear very much in everyday conversation—maybe more familiar words we should use for the purposes of this topic are *manage* and *management.*

Jesus said, "To find your life you must lose it." I believe that to understand and live as God's steward is the most liberating lifestyle you could have. It's much better than the world's way of living just for yourself. Imagine the pressure you would be under if you held it all and everything relied on you. Placing your life into God's hands is true freedom!

Understanding the idea of stewardship (management) really begins with this question: *Who owns the stuff?* The Bible has a lot to say about this, but here's one verse that pretty much sums it all up:

> **The earth is the Lord's, and everything in it,**
> **the world, and all who live in it.**
>
> **Psalm 24:1 NIV**

God is the owner, and we are the managers. That's the picture of stewardship we see in the Bible. For most people, this is a major change in perspective. We all start off in our sin nature (our flesh), having difficulty understanding this. We think we worked for all that stuff, so it belongs to us. But that's absolutely wrong! God owns it all, but He trusts us to manage what belongs to Him.

Not too long ago I took my oldest daughter to Chick-fil-A for lunch. Although I really like their chicken, that's not the reason I go there to eat. I have to be honest with you. I take my daughters to Chick-fil-A because I really love their waffle fries! *(I know they're a little fattening with the oil and all the carbs, but to me, they're heavenly!)* I take my kids there often, and do you know what happens every single time? My girls never finish their food. To be more specific, they never finish their fries. *(Which is awesome because that means there are more for me!)*

Well, one time when my oldest daughter and I were there, I ordered a chicken sandwich, but I didn't order any fries because she had fries with her kids' meal, and she never finishes them. I remember we were sitting there that day just having a great time together. She had finished the chicken nuggets I paid for and was licking her ice cream cone, which I bought for her. But she had only eaten half of the fries from her meal. As I was reaching forward to grab some fries, my six-year-old daughter slapped my hand and said, "Those are my fries, Papa!"

Now, I had to take a moment of silence and just breathe. *(Remember, I pastor a church.)* As I calmed my temper, I realized this was an opportune moment to pastor my own child, and I said, "What do you mean they're your fries, honey? I'm the one who bought those fries. As a matter of fact, I have the power to make sure you don't ever have any fries again. I'm your Papa. I bought those fries, and they're mine." Then I reached for one.

And did my lesson on stewardship work?

Absolutely NOT!

She smacked my hand again and said, "These are my fries, Papa! They're mine."

So much for my pastoring skills! I obviously still had some work to do.

You know, we laugh at that kind of childlike innocence, but let's remember that we also get things very wrong at times. **We can mentally agree that God owns everything, but then act as though He doesn't.**

God is a good parent, and like any good parent, what do we want for our kids? Do we just want their fries? Of course not! We want our kids to be better. We want them to learn. We want them to receive and use all the good gifts we have for them. Our Heavenly Papa is the same way.

Everything on this planet belongs to God. That includes you and me.

Here's the most important principle we can learn about stewardship: We must manage our time, abilities, and finances God's way to become better.

THE PARABLE OF THE TALENTS

Let's look at a very famous parable that Jesus told His disciples:

> **Again, it will be like a man going on a journey, who called his servants and entrusted his wealth to them. To one he gave five bags of gold, to another two bags, and to another one bag, each according to his ability. Then he went on his journey. The man who had received five bags of gold went at once and put his money to work and gained five bags more.**
>
> **Matthew 25:14–16 NIV**

This story is about how these stewards managed their master's money. The master owned it all, but what made these stewards different from each other wasn't how much they originally got or even how much they eventually earned. It was **how they used their time** to manage what they were given.

You've probably heard the saying, "Time is money." Maybe you've scoffed at that, but it is a fact. You *literally* trade your time for money. You give your employer or your own business your hours each week, and you get a paycheck in exchange.

This is interesting to note, but there's a concept that you'll never find in the Bible: the concept of fairness. Look, he gave one bag, two bags, five bags—*that doesn't seem fair!* Why did the master give different amounts of money to each person? Because we're all different. We have different gifts and callings. We have different potential. **God promotes the concept of fruitfulness, not fairness.**

Thank goodness, we're not responsible for what God gives to someone else, but we are responsible for what He entrusts to us. That's how the kingdom works.

If you don't know the end of the story, let me just summarize it for you. The man with the five bags of money invested it and made five more bags. The man with two bags made two more, and the guy who only had one bag to start with buried it in the ground and didn't do anything.

There are two things we can learn from this story.

1. **God holds us accountable.**

   The owner in the story came back to account for how his servants had handled what they were given—not for what was given to the person next to them, but for what they were each given personally. One day, you and I will stand before God in the same place. On that day, it will be clear that **God rewards fruitfulness.**

   Some people think that God rewards faithfulness. But that's not entirely true. **You can be faithfully doing**

the wrong things *(like the servant with the single bag of money)* **and end up with nothing in the end.**

You can be faithful to work eighty hours a week, but in the end, you'll lose your family.

You can be faithful to attend church, but if you aren't helping to reach people for Jesus or to build the kingdom, you'll miss the amazing blessings of God that are happening all around you.

We must never allow ourselves to become selfish or to become paralyzed with fear, or we will miss God's amazing rewards. God holds us accountable for what He's given us to steward.

2. **God wants us to invest wisely.**

    God wants us to invest in the spiritual realm—not just in the things of this natural world. God wants us to use the time, talents, and resources He has trusted us with to reach people with the Gospel.

    If you only bury God's resources in the dirt of this world—for your own pleasure or out of fear—you have invested poorly.

    Make no mistake: Where you decide to spend your natural resources—your time, talents, and money—is a spiritual decision. Invest them wisely.

WHERE DOES THE TIME GO?

When you think about the topic of stewardship, most people automatically think it's mostly about how we manage money. But that's not really the key focus of stewardship. To be sure, it does include the subject of wise money management, but stewardship is really more about how you handle your time. *(Again, time is money.)*

We all think we need more time, but what we really need is practical wisdom to be better stewards of the time God has already given us.

With that in mind, here are a few tips for becoming a better manager of your time.

SOME PRACTICAL WISDOM FOR BETTER TIME MANAGEMENT

1. **Start with the big stuff first**.

   Don't allow the "urgent" to run your life. Move toward your personal vision. (We talked about finding your personal vision in the last chapter.)

   Use a "funnel-down" approach for how you schedule your life. Start with the big things—what's most important—and always give them your time first.

   God

   Your spouse

   Your children

   Your connection to spiritual family, your local church

   Your career

   Don't let the smaller, less important things crowd out your time with God, your family, or your church.

2. **Audit your time.**

   Yes, like the IRS might audit your finances, you need to audit your time. Many people are scared of the word "audit." *(I'm a little scared of it, too. I've been audited before, and it's scary.)* But in the same way the IRS might audit your finances, you need to audit your time.

Do you want more resources? Be a better time manager.

› Look ahead—Quarterly planning is wise.

› Think about your week before your week starts. A good architect makes up plans before the construction starts.

› Think about your day before it starts. Be sure to schedule your time to connect with God each day.

› At the end of each day, journal and reflect on what happened and how you can improve tomorrow.

3. Ask God for wisdom.

There will be many times when you don't know what to do.

Teach us to number [schedule] our days, that we may gain a heart of wisdom.

Psalm 90:12 NIV [Author's Note]

Remember our study in chapter three? We must let our lives be driven by faith. A child of God cannot be a victim of the world. Ask God for wisdom, and believe that He'll give you everything you need to accomplish everything He's called you to do. Only God holds our destiny in His hands. Ask Him for guidance, and take time to listen.

4. Hustle.

Do you know what hustle is? Hustle is work. *Work* is a four-letter word, but it's not a bad word. Work is good. Do you realize when Jesus comes back, you're still going to have to work? You're going to have responsibility and oversee things. You're going to rule and reign with Him.

Do not merely listen to the word, and so deceive yourselves. Do what it says.

James 1:22 NIV

God will give you wisdom. He will speak to you through His Word, through circumstances, in prayer, through others, even when you're in the shower.... And when He speaks, hustle! *(In Matthew 25:16 it says the wise steward "went at once.")*

When we learn to steward our time, abilities, and finances God's way we will become better and receive His reward.

KEY THOUGHT
You must manage your time, abilities, and finances God's way to become better.

CHAPTER NOTES

KEY THOUGHT

You must manage
your time, abilities, and
finances God's way
to become better.

CHAPTER 6
A Better Steward

SMALL GROUP AND DEVOTIONAL LESSONS

READ

Jesus said if you want to find your life, you must lose it. That doesn't necessarily mean Jesus is asking you to be a martyr, but He is asking you to live for Him. He's asking you to put all your resources on the line for Him and to steward them wisely. **Living as a steward is living with the understanding that God owns it all, and you are only a manager of the things He has entrusted to you.**

Living with the mindset of a steward is the most liberating lifestyle you could have. It's so much higher and better than the world's way of living only for yourself. **We can mentally agree that God owns everything, but then act as though He doesn't.** But God owns everything on this planet, including you.

To become better, you must manage your time, abilities, and finances God's way. You aren't responsible for what God gives to someone else, but you are responsible for what He entrusts to you. One day we'll all give an account to God for how we managed what He put in our care. God rewards fruitfulness. Steward your time and resources with His priorities, and ask Him for wisdom to accomplish His purposes here on the Earth.

☐ **DAY 1** **Matthew 25:14–30 and Acts 15**

☐ **DAY 2** **James 1:16–18 and Acts 16**

☐ **DAY 3** **Proverbs 3:9 and Acts 17**

☐ **DAY 4** **Psalm 90:12–17 and Acts 18**

☐ **DAY 5** **2 Corinthians 9:6–7 and Acts 19**

☐ **DAY 6** **Ephesians 5:15–17 and Acts 20**

☐ **DAY 7** **Colossians 4:5 and Acts 21**

REFLECT

1. What does stewardship mean to you? Since you are a steward of everything you have been given, how would you rate yourself as manager of your time, finances, relationships, and abilities?

2. Identify some areas in your life that you can steward better. How can you become better in those areas?

WRITE

Journal your thoughts from the discussion questions here.

CHAPTER 7

Fully Devoted

Wouldn't it be amazing if God showed up one day at your house just to hang out? I know Jesus is always with us, but wouldn't it be cool if He just walked into your house (bodily) today?

He'd just walk through the wall of course *(because He can do that)*. He wouldn't need you to open the door!

What if He just walked in and sat down on your couch and started watching the game, or something?

"Hey, Stephen. Please pass the chips and salsa. Oh, praise Me! I just knew the quarterback was going to throw that touchdown!"

Seriously—wouldn't that be awesome?!

Do you know that God wants to have a close personal friendship with you like that?

Well, maybe He's not going to come sit on your couch and watch the game, but He does want to have a deep friendship with you because He really loves you and cares about you as His son or daughter.

He wants to hang out with you and have a close relationship with you and help you to become better in every area of your life.

So why is it that we often feel as if God is far away?

"I got laid off at work today, God."

"I just found out my mother has cancer, Lord."

"My best friend isn't talking to me anymore, Jesus."

"GOD, WHERE ARE YOU?"

Have you ever felt that God is distant?

In this chapter, we're going to wrap up our journey to becoming better as we come full circle to learn that God's best for our lives involves **a close personal relationship** and **an intimate friendship** with Him.

Let's take a look at a verse in the Bible that many people misread.

> Come near to God and he will come near to you.
>
> James 4:8a NIV

The problem is that most people have it backward. Most people think, *If God would just show Himself to me, then I would follow Him.*

They pray "foxhole" prayers. "Lord, if You'll just do this, I'll serve You with my whole heart." "Just show me a sign, Lord, and I'll serve You forever."

But that's *NOT* what James 4:8 says. It says we need to come close to Him, and *THEN* He will draw near to us.

Here's what they're missing: God already came to us.

Jesus came to Earth for us. He took on a human body, was born as a baby, lived here in the flesh for about thirty-three years, died on a cross for our sins, and then was raised from the dead—all so we could live an abundant life—a better life in close personal relationship with Him.

He *already* came down.

Once we accept His sacrifice and become born again, it's **our turn** to do the drawing near. The Bible says, if we will draw near to Him, **He'll come as close as we'll let Him be to us in our lives.**

Something you need to know about Jesus is that He isn't a bully. He's not going to push His way into your life. He's not going to force you to go somewhere you don't want to go or to do something you don't want to do.

God is fully devoted to us. And we need to understand what it means to be fully devoted to Him.

HOW OUR RELATIONSHIP WITH GOD WORKS

It is important that you understand how a relationship with Jesus works.

God's work in our lives is past, present, and future: God exists outside of time. God is present just as much in our past as He is in our present as He is in our future. I know that sounds confusing, so I'll break it down.

» **He's in our past.** There's the moment when we first believed. We gave our lives to Jesus, and we were born again. Our sins were forgiven, and we were set free from the past. Sin no longer has a hold on us.

> **Sin is no longer your master, for you no longer live under the requirements of the law. Instead, you live under the freedom of God's grace.**
>
> **Romans 6:14 NLT**

This is the starting place we talked about in the first chapter of this book.

I want to re-emphasize this: *You can never be everything you were designed to be apart from a personal relationship with Jesus.*

» **He's in our future.** Christ is working in our future. Did you know that Jesus is preparing a place for us?

> **My Father's house has many rooms…. And if I go and prepare a place for you, I will come back and take you to be with me that you also may be where I am.**
>
> John 14:2–3 NIV

Jesus is working on our future, but while we are in this current age, our world is hindered by sin, decay, and death. The Bible says in 1 Corinthians 15:26 that the last enemy to be destroyed is death. Jesus is preparing a place for us in the future that will be free from the consequences of death and sin. Not only has Jesus forgiven our past, He's at work right now preparing our future.

And what about our present? The here and now?

» **He is present in our present.** From that moment when we were born again, a new life began for us. But that was only the start of our journey with God.

> **Therefore, if anyone is in Christ, the new creation has come: The old has gone, the new is here!**
>
> 2 Corinthians 5:17 NIV

When we decide to follow Christ and are born again, our spirits become new, and we have a relationship with God. **But we don't know His ways yet.** That doesn't happen overnight. Similar to any new relationship we have, it takes us time to learn about the other person.

Recently I spent some time with people who knew me before I became a Christian. I've served Jesus for years, and, honestly, I am a different person now. They knew me before Christ changed my life, and they were amazed at the transformation they saw in me. But the change in me didn't happen overnight. It happened over the last twenty-five years of allowing Him to work in me.

I'm so thankful God accepted me the way He found me, and I'm even more thankful He didn't leave me there. Although I'm not where I used to be, I'm not where God wants me to be yet. I still have some work to do. I still need to devote myself fully to becoming better and drawing closer to Him.

PUTTING IN THE HARD WORK

Now here's the final principle I want to wrap this book up with. *(Don't miss this!)* **Being fully devoted to God means doing the hard work of putting Him first in every area of our lives.**

> **Don't copy the behavior and customs of this world, but let God transform you into a new person by changing the way you think. Then you will learn to know God's will for you, which is good and pleasing and perfect.**
>
> **Romans 12:2 NLT**

We live in such a fast-moving, fast-thinking, fast-food world that this can sometimes come as a shock to us. When we pray to accept Jesus, our journey isn't over. It's just beginning. There's more to it—more to learn, to do, and to discover.

> ...I have come that they may have life, and have it to the full.
>
> John 10:10b NIV

We could translate the word Jesus used for *full* in that verse as *your best life now.*

Many believers have been saved from their past. They've been forgiven, and Jesus is preparing a future for them in Heaven, but they don't ever step into their best possible lives. They never reach the potential God has for them.

Why? Because they aren't fully devoted to grow in their faith right here and now.

Growing closer and more devoted to God is a life-long journey. It doesn't happen in an instant. It takes time. It comes one step at a time.

> **The Lord makes firm the steps of the one who delights in him. Though he may stumble, he will not fall, for the Lord upholds him with his hand.**
>
> Psalm 37:23–24 NIV

I'm so glad God doesn't expect me to be perfect. I'm glad His grace makes room for me to grow into all that He has for me. There's room for me to make mistakes and to continue to push forward.

> **In their hearts humans plan their course, but the Lord establishes their steps.**
>
> Proverbs 16:9 NIV

> **Guide my steps by your word, so I will not be overcome by evil.**
>
> Psalm 119:133 NLT

God leads us in steps. That's what being fully devoted is all about. It's about **doing the little things that have a big impact** and make us **better**. *Not perfect, but better!*

RUN THE RACE

Look at what the Apostle Paul wrote to Christians about being fully devoted.

> **Do you not know that in a race all the runners run, but only one gets the prize? Run in such a way as to get the prize. Everyone who competes in the games goes into strict training. They do it to get a crown that will not last, but we do it to get a crown that will last forever.**
>
> **1 Corinthians 9:24–25 NIV**

There are so many marathoners in the church that I pastor. And I can tell you, when they're training, it does *NOT* look like fun! They look like they're starving. They're running for hours, and they're working out all the time. It isn't fun to train, but they're training for the real fun. Do you know what the real fun is? The real fun is winning!

God likes to win, too. Cover to cover, the Bible is the story of God winning: winning in the world, winning against the forces of darkness, winning in our lives, winning in making us better.

I recently started working out with a coach who gave me a training program. And, at first, it was terrible. Honestly, I don't like the gym. I don't like going there. I don't like to sweat. I just look at runners, and I get tired, and I want to take a nap. I remember when my coach first gave me this training plan. It was like I was a baby to working out. I had no experience. My body was weak. I had to start out with really light weights. It was embarrassing! But as I began to be fully devoted to the program, I started to get stronger. It took nearly six months for me to start actually feeling better.

There is a spiritual training program that positions you to be strong so that you can run your race and win. It won't get you there overnight. In fact, it will take your full devotion for your whole life to complete it, but it's worth it to win in the end.

GOD'S TRAINING PROGRAM

Each of these exercises are backed by a one-hundred-percent, "get better" guarantee by God to help us to grow closer to Him so we can fulfill His design for our lives.

They are proven to make us better. *(If you don't get better, you're not fully devoted to them.)* You'll never rise to an occasion, but you will always fall to the level of your preparation. Success is not a fluke in your relationship with God. If you draw near to God, He will draw near to you.

» **Exercise 1: Bible Study**

There is only one way to get to know God. You must know His Word, the Bible.

> **For the word of God is alive and active. Sharper than any double-edged sword, it penetrates even to dividing soul and spirit, joints and marrow; it judges the thoughts and attitudes of the heart.**
>
> **Hebrews 4:12 NIV**

God's Word is alive. You get to know Jesus by knowing the Bible.

Here are some basics about studying the Bible:

› **Read and meditate on God's Word.** When you're reading, memorizing, and giving focused attention to learning God's Word, you begin to know who He is and how He works.

› **Listen to and hear God's Word.** Romans 10:17 says faith comes from hearing God's Word. When you go to church and hear God's Word, your faith is built for life.

› **Speak God's Word.** Jesus always spoke God's Word. (See Matthew 4.) The only thing that overcomes a lie from the enemy is a truth from

God's Word. There is power when God's Word is spoken.

» **Exercise 2: Prayer**

Prayer is simply talking to God. Many people never grow in their relationship with God because they never talk to God. They never hear from God because they never engage Him in conversation.

What would happen if you didn't talk to your wife or children for a year? Chances are you would drift away from them relationally. If we're going to know God's plan for our lives, we need to talk to Him and let Him talk to us.

> **Trust in him at all times, you people; pour out your hearts to him, for God is our refuge.**
>
>

Psalm 62:8 NIV

Here are some basics when it comes to prayer:

› **Just start.** Pour out your heart to God. What's on your mind? What are you thankful for? What's keeping you up at night? 1 Peter 5:7 encourages us to take our cares and worries to Him because He cares about us.

› **Pray God's Word.** Not sure what to say? Just speak God's Word. Pray scriptures over yourself and your circumstances. God's Word never fails. The Bible is alive and active. Use it!

› **Pray with others.** Prayer is a team sport. Jesus says in Matthew 18:19 that where two or more believers are gathered together, they can ask anything in His name, and they will receive it. There is power in numbers. Get your small group involved. There is so much power when we agree in prayer with our spiritual family.

» **Exercise 3: Worship**

While worship can be Bible study and prayer, in the big picture, it's the overall honor and adoration of God. Worship is more than just singing some songs. It's a lifestyle that honors and prioritizes God and puts His will first.

> **Therefore, I urge you, brothers and sisters, in view of God's mercy, to offer your bodies as a living sacrifice, holy and pleasing to God—this is your true and proper worship.**
>
> **Romans 12:1 NIV**

As I said before, many people brag about what they would do for God. In the moment of trouble, they say they would give up their lives for God. But God probably isn't asking you to die for Him today. **He's asking you to be a living sacrifice that other people can see.** When people see God at work in your life, through your worship and devotion, it draws them closer to Him.

Here are some basics concerning worship:

› **Sabbath Rest.** God designed us to work and rest. The Sabbath is right up there in the Ten Commandments with "do not murder" and "do not lie," yet so many people don't take time to rest and reflect, to consider God in their toil and work. We worship God when we make time for the Sabbath. The biblical duration of a sabbath is sun up to sun down every seventh day. Schedule some white space into your life. It will make you better. As we step away from the busyness of life, we can see and hear Him more clearly.

› **Sing songs and hymns.** There is something about singing that unlocks surrender to God in the human heart. We are admonished in Colossians 3:16 to build each other up with songs and hymns. In James 5:13, we're encouraged to pray and sing praises to God even when we're suffering. In times of trouble, songs of worship help us remember how good, strong, and powerful God is. It clears our minds and helps our spirits to focus in on His presence, no matter what we may be facing. Music connects us to God in a supernatural way.

› **Worship with spiritual family.** Growing alongside others in God's family builds us up. We grow in our gifts and in our maturity alongside people who want more *FOR* us than *FROM* us. Hebrews 10:25 tells us we should not forsake getting together with other members of God's spiritual family. We should be encouraging one another even more, as we see the time of the Lord's return is getting nearer. As I mentioned before, our faith is personal, but it was never meant to be private. We can't do this alone. It's impossible for us to become all that God wants us to be apart from spiritual family.

As we fully devote ourselves to God through studying the Bible, through prayer, and through worship, we will change and grow one step at a time. Our sin won't get worked off. It will just fall off.

As we keep our eyes fixed on Christ, who is the Author and Perfecter of our faith, we'll draw near to Him, and He will draw near to us. **And the closer we walk to Jesus, the better we'll become.**

The things that weighed us down in the past—our old sin nature, the wrong thoughts and beliefs we had, our selfish habits, they'll all fall away, and we'll be transformed one step at a time.

KEY THOUGHT

Being fully devoted to God means putting Him first in every area of your life.

CHAPTER NOTES

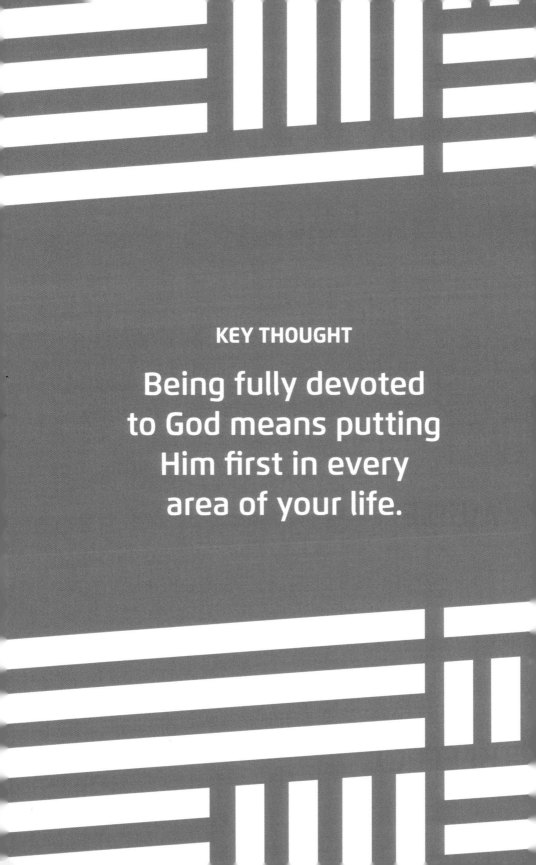

KEY THOUGHT

Being fully devoted
to God means putting
Him first in every
area of your life.

CHAPTER 7
Fully Devoted

SMALL GROUP AND DEVOTIONAL LESSONS

READ

God wants to have a close personal relationship with you to help you become better. **Sometimes we may feel as if God is far away, but God promised to draw near to us when we draw near to Him.** Jesus came to Earth, died on the cross, and was raised from the dead so that we could live an abundant life. He is fully devoted to you, and you must become fully devoted to Him.

Having a close personal relationship with God doesn't just happen overnight. It takes a lot of time to get to know God on a deep and personal level. In fact, it will take your entire lifetime. When you pray to accept Christ as your Savior, your journey has only just begun. There is so much more! True life change only happens one step at a time.

Studying the Bible and speaking it increases your faith. Prayer, both alone and with others, brings the answers you need and the power of agreement into your life. And worshiping God with your whole life alongside spiritual family brings maturity to make you better. **As you draw near to God through His Word, by prayer, and in worship, you will be transformed and become better day by day.**

☐ **DAY 1**   **Romans 12:1–5 and Acts 22**

☐ **DAY 2**   **1 Corinthians 9:24–27 and Acts 23**

☐ **DAY 3**   **James 1:5–8 and Acts 24**

☐ **DAY 4**   **James 5:16-28 and Acts 25**

☐ **DAY 5**   **James 1:19–27 and Acts 26**

☐ **DAY 6**   **2 Timothy 3:16–17 and Acts 27**

☐ **DAY 7**   **Hebrews 4:12 and Acts 28**

REFLECT

1. What does your relationship with God look like in your day-to-day life? What do you think is the most important component of a healthy relationship with God?

2. How would you rate yourself in the spiritual disciplines of prayer, worship, and Bible reading? What can you do to be more consistent in these essential disciplines?

WRITE

Journal your thoughts from the discussion questions here.

CONCLUSION

Over the years, as I've applied each of the principles found in this book, there have been times when I've felt frustrated with my own progress. I've felt as if I wasn't good enough or advancing fast enough. I've always struggled with striving toward my idea of perfection, only to fall short and feel like a failure. It was during one of these low moments that an older, more experienced believer encouraged me to avoid looking at my life as a series of separated events, but instead to look at it as if it were a picture that God is painting. This friend reminded me that God is perfect, and He doesn't make mistakes. He encouraged me to trust God with the final outcome of the picture and to continue taking steps toward *better*.

That's the big idea of this entire book. ***Better* is about progress, not perfection.**

Better isn't a destination. It's a journey that will last the rest of your life. The principles found in this book haven't made me perfect by any means, but they have made me better.

Think of each principle presented as the starting line for lasting growth in every area of your life. You will likely have to revisit each of the principles at various times on your journey to *better*.

Here are some closing thoughts for each principle:

Better isn't in us, It's in Jesus.

You will never be all that God has called you to be apart from a personal relationship with Jesus. When you feel stressed or overwhelmed in your journey to better, always remember that God is faithful. He will never leave you. He is good.

Becoming better starts with letting your spirit lead.

Better doesn't happen from your own strength. You must continue to nurture and feed your spirit. It's the part of you that connects with God. When you are strong spiritually, you're prepared for anything that comes your way, and you will see how God can use even the toughest of circumstances to make you better.

What you believe about God and yourself changes everything.

Cultivate a perspective that makes God and His power big in your life. Fear, anger, and hopelessness have no power over you when you believe what the Bible says about you and about God. There is freedom in God's design for you, and you can only discover that design in the Bible. Commit to getting to know God by knowing His Word. When you're confused and don't know what to do, always go back to what you *do* know, God is good, and He is faithful. The Holy Spirit will guide you as you study the Bible, and your faith will grow.

To make us better, God brings us together.

You only fail one way—*alone*. Invest in life-giving relationships. The best relationships aren't those that echo your own opinions and observations, but those that challenge you. Surround yourself with people who want more *for* you than *from* you. You need spiritual family to help you grow into your God-given destiny. Without it you will always struggle with your identity and true purpose.

What you see makes you better.

What you set your eyes on will draw you toward it. Your life will move toward the picture you see. If you want to change direction, set your eyes on something better. Involve God in the process, and allow Him to grow and expand your vision over time. Always think big picture and work your way down to the details. This will guarantee that you end up somewhere on purpose.

You must manage your time, abilities, and finances God's way to become better.

Each of us has the same amount of time as anyone else. It's how we use that time that matters. Many times throughout your journey you'll be tempted to replace the important with the urgent. Don't fall for this trap. Instead, audit your time as if it were the most valuable resource you have—because it is. Manage all the resources God has entrusted to you wisely.

Being fully devoted to God means putting Him first in every area of your life.

Ultimately, we all have to choose our paths, and the journey to *better* isn't easy. It will take discipline, patience, and perseverance in the face of adversity to get there. Anything of great value comes at a great cost. Determine in your heart to pay the price to become better. It's worth it.

Let me just encourage you today. **You can be better.** God designed you to succeed and to live a life greater than you could ever imagine. Don't give up. Don't give in. **You've got this!**

***Better* is within your reach because of Jesus.**

A PRAYER FOR SALVATION

Jesus,

I need You. I am tired of living my way, and I want to choose Your better way. Please help me. I invite You into my life to be my Lord and Savior. I believe what the Bible says about You is true. You are God. You came from Heaven to Earth. You lived a perfect life, and You died on the cross to forgive my sin, my failures, and my mistakes. I believe that three days after You were crucified, You rose from the dead and defeated death forever. I put my hope and trust in Your resurrection power. Come into my heart, and be my Lord and Savior. Change my life with the power of Your Holy Spirit. Thank You for meeting me where I am and for showing me a better way to live.

Amen.

OTHER RECOMMENDED RESOURCES

The **Better Planner**™ is a thirteen-week personal planner designed to help you map out all the different aspects of success and personal growth on your way to *better*.

It can get complicated to make sure you're doing all the right things in all the right areas of life, but the **Better Planner**™ cuts through all the confusing apps and habit trackers, and puts the path to personal development right into the palm of your hands.

The **Better Planner**™ is radically different in its approach. By incorporating the seven biblical principles found in the book **Better: My Life. God's Design.** into one easy-to-use, thirteen-week planner, the **Better Planner**™ provides a framework for you to achieve success and follow God's plan for your life.

The foundation of the **Better Planner**™ is the practice of defining and reaching your personal vision. The other principles for growth all integrate with and flow out of this essential step. As you develop and record the insights you receive from God and His design for your life, the **Better Planner**™ will lead you through a step-by-step process to become better.

To start your journey to *better*, order your copy of the **Better Planner**™ at *betterplanner.com* today!

SPECIAL THANKS

When I first gave my life to Jesus as an eleven-year-old boy, I could never have imagined how richly he would bless my future through divine relationships. These relationships were built on the solid foundation of faith in Jesus and have been monumental in my personal journey to *better* and in developing the content in this book.

Kyla. Thank you for saying "yes" and believing in our life together. Your love, encouragement, and patience have made me better in every area of life. I love you and attribute any success as our success. I love the life we're building together with our beautiful children, Adilyn, Breelyn, and Greyson!

Lon and Stephanie Martin. Thank you for taking me into your family as a young man and for modeling unconditional love, generosity, and hard work. The lessons you taught me have served me well in loving and leading others.

Pastor Willie George and Church On The Move. Thank you for your leadership. I accepted Christ and learned how to hear God, read the Bible, and lead in ministry at Church On The Move. Your example and your words of wisdom have given me a greater confidence in the power of God's Word and His call on my life.

Pastor Jeff Little. Thank you for being my pastor, my coach, and my spiritual dad. Thank you for pushing me to grow and develop into my God-given potential and for believing in me even when I didn't believe in myself. It is one of my greatest honors to build the local church with you and our spiritual family of churches.

Vintage Church. Thank you for being the best church a pastor could ask for. Your love for people and your commitment to our mission to reach people and build lives inspires me daily. It is an honor to love and lead alongside each of you!

Scott McBride, Jon Scott, Gary and Barb Rosberg, Joe Torres. Thank you for coaching and encouraging me to be a better Christ-follower, husband, pastor, leader, and friend.

Linda Schantz. Thank you for helping me write and edit ***Better.*** I had no idea how to put what was in my heart onto a page, but you used your skill and stayed committed to the project and made it all possible.

ABOUT THE AUTHOR

Stephen Martin has been in ministry, serving the local church for more than twenty years. Born and raised in Tulsa, Oklahoma, Stephen began serving in ministry as a teenager, and then as an intern at his hometown church, Church On The Move. He went on to help with a local church plant and earn a bachelor's degree in interdisciplinary studies from Lindenwood University in Saint Louis, Missouri.

Stephen is passionate about serving and resourcing the local church—specifically church leaders. In 2009, he started One Church Resource, a global, online, sharing network for pastors, church leaders, and creatives.

In 2013, Stephen and his family moved to Texas and planted Vintage Church just outside of Fort Hood, the largest military base in the United States. Today, Vintage Church is a church of thousands and continues to make a significant impact in the Central Texas region. As the founder and Senior Pastor of this vibrant, growing congregation, Stephen firmly believes in its mission of *Reaching People* and *Building Lives.* He is dedicated to helping others take steps to grow into their God-given potential.

When he's not pastoring people or coaching leaders, Stephen loves spending time with his family, hunting deer, and reading. Stephen's wife, Kyla, is a Family Medicine Physician in the United States Army, and they have two beautiful daughters, Adilyn and Breelyn, and a son, Greyson.